Published by
Gallery Books
An imprint of W H Smith Publishers Inc.
112 Madison Avenue
New York, New York 10016 USA

Produced by
Twin Books
15 Sherwood Place
Greenwich, CT 06830 USA

© 1991 The Walt Disney Company

ISBN 0-8317-2303-3

Printed in Hong Kong

Fun with Words
In the Country

Twin Books

GALLERY BOOKS
An imprint of W.H. Smith Publishers Inc.
112 Madison Avenue
New York, New York 10016

750

ON THE FARM

The Disney Babies are staying on a farm with a   high on a hill. At first Baby Goofy

was frightened by the  , but he likes

to watch the hens walk down the little ramp from

the henhouse. Baby Pete just likes to sit and

smell the hay. Soon it will be stacked in the big

red  . Baby Mickey has found

a friendly little bee who brings him fresh honey

straight from the  . Behind him is the

place where the farmer gets water for the farm.

The bucket has fallen off the  .

Barn

Scarecrow

Windmill

Well

Beehive

ANIMALS ON THE FARM

The Disney Babies like all the animals on the

farm, even the chickens and the

who wakes them up. Baby Gyro is sitting high up

on the back of the  . He would like to

ride. Baby Daisy is wondering if she could learn

to milk a  . Baby Donald is surprised :

someone has taken a bite out of his book ! It's not

the little  . He is still sitting by his

trough, waiting for something to eat. Who is

chewing on the page ? It's the naughty little

. Which animal do you like best ?

Rooster

Horse

Cow

Pig

Goat

BABIES ON THE FARM

There always seem to be baby animals on a

farm. Baby Gyro is trying to count them.

One is a little  who stands in front

of him, but something is blowing on his neck.

Is it the  ? Baby Gyro turns around to

see who is behind him. Why, it's a woolly

 . Baby Minnie is also making friends.

She can't decide which one she likes best.

The  in front of her wants to play,

but he might be a little rough. The gentle

is waiting her turn.

Calf

Lamb

Kitten

Foal

Puppy

A COUNTRY BREAKFAST

Every morning when the Disney Babies are on

the farm, they have a big breakfast. Baby Horace

likes to eat his soft-boiled  right out

of the shell in an egg cup. Baby Gus has found

a slice of ripe 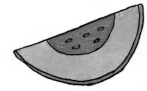 . The table is filled

with other good food, including milk, butter

and  . Baby Pete is on the floor. He is

teasing Baby Pluto, pretending to give him a slice

of  . Baby Clarabelle is eating her favorite

breakfast, covered with syrup. It's a big stack of

 . What do you like for breakfast ?

Melon

Egg

Jam

Pancakes

Bacon

THE VEGETABLE GARDEN

The  are ripe, and the Disney Babies are

supposed to be picking them, but look at Baby

Pete. He's taking a nap in the 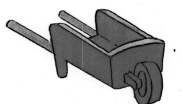.

He doesn't like vegetables anyway. Baby Donald

is picking , but he's eating them

straight off the vine. Someone else in the garden

is hungry. A little mole is munching on a .

Baby Minnie and Baby Mickey are playing hide

and seek. Baby Minnie has hidden herself in a

, but Baby Mickey has found her

at last, next to a big orange pumpkin.

Beans

Tomatoes

Wheelbarrow

Carrot

Cabbage

THE ORCHARD

Some of the Disney Babies are playing in the

orchard. Baby Clarabelle is cutting

right off the vine. Baby Gyro is towing boxes

of fruit, including some delicious 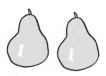 ,

with his tricycle. The last wagon contains sweet

red  . Some small animals are also

storing nuts and fruit. One bold little mouse has

found a that dropped out of a box.

Baby Gus has had a surprise. He was sitting

under a tree when a big ripe  fell right

on his head. Ouch! Did that hurt!

Apple

Grapes

Cherries

Pears

Plum

THE FLOWER GARDEN

It's a beautiful sunny day and the Disney Babies

are playing in a garden filled with flowers.

Baby Mickey has picked a  especially for

Baby Minnie, because it is her favorite.

She is sunbathing under a  which is as

golden as the sun itself. Poor Baby Pete has

tripped and fallen into a bed of . Baby

Daisy has her favorite flower, too. She likes the

 because the color is so pretty, and she

thinks each one has a little face. She tried to pick

one, but it flew away. It really was a  .

Butterfly

Tulips

Pansy

Sunflower

Rose

IN THE FIELD

The  is ripe and ready to harvest, so the

Disney Babies are joining the fun. Baby Daisy is

having a wonderful time on top of the

throwing down forkfuls of hay. Baby Horace

would rather pound on the stakes that hold the

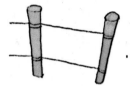 . Baby Gyro thinks he has the best job.

He loves to drive the little  around

and around. But Baby Goofy is happiest of all.

He is sitting in the field of  and is about

to take a bite. He may be sorry when he finds out

it isn't cooked and there isn't any butter.

Fence

Haystack

Corn

Tractor

Wheat

A COUNTRY FAIR

There are so many wonderful things to do

at a country fair. Baby Donald and Baby

Mickey are at the  , pretending

to race. Baby Gus has decided he can judge

the best 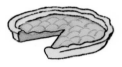 in the baked-goods booth.

Then he thinks it could be even better to taste a

doughnut. After that, he might have

to have some cake, and some muffins. The

 looks good, too. Baby Pete thought

he was looking at a , but

that's Baby Minnie peering through the frame.

Photograph

Bread

Pie

Pony Ride

SPRING

It's spring, and everything in the garden,

including the  , is growing quickly.

Baby Clarabelle wonders how it happens. The

Babies look at each opening . The sun

has gone behind a cloud, and a gentle spring

 has started to fall. Baby Minnie doesn't

mind the rain, because she remembered to bring

her big  . Baby Pete is very happy

because he has an enormous puddle to

play in. Look ! All the Babies can see the

beautiful through the shower.

SUMMER

What a lovely summer day ! The 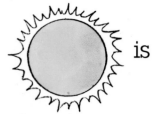 is

shining and the Disney Babies are having

a picnic. Baby Mickey is a bit surprised :

The  are stealing his sandwich !

Baby Gus is taking a little nap after lunch

and a delicious  . Baby Donald

is enjoying the garden. He likes to look

at the tall  and the roses.

He is worried that the flowers are not

getting enough water and has brought his

 . What do you like about summer ?

Sun

Glass of Lemonade

Ants

Hollyhocks

Watering Can

FALL

The weather is changing and it is getting

cold. Each Disney Baby wears a  to

keep warm outside. Baby Daisy wears a

woolen  as well. The leaves

are changing color and beginning to fall.

Baby Daisy and Baby Gyro are playing in a big

pile of leaves. A  sits in the

tree above them. He would like to play, too.

Baby Horace has a  and is pulling

together another leaf pile. When he is finished, all

the Disney Babies can jump in the  .

Squirrel

Jacket

Muffler

Leaves

Rake

WINTER

It has snowed, and the Disney Babies have

built a great  to play with. Baby

Pete is hiding behind the snowman and making a

 . He is planning to throw it

at Baby Minnie, who is driving in

a little  pulled by a reindeer.

Baby Donald and Baby Daisy are racing down

the snowy hill on a new  . Playing

in the snow is great fun, especially if you are

wearing warm clothes and have thick

 to keep your hands warm.

Snowman

Snowball

Sleigh

Sled

Mittens

IN THE WOODS

The Disney Babies are taking a walk in the

woods, and have met several little animals.

Baby Goofy has found a baby  . "Don't

try to pat him", says Goofy's new friend, the wise

red  . "His spines can be very sharp

and prickly", adds the little striped

 . A young bird has flown down

to sit on Baby Mickey's hand, while another

 stays in the nest. Baby Clarabelle is

happy just picking some of the flowers. The

 is her favorite.

Fox

Chipmunk

Lily-of-the-valley

Porcupine

Bird

IN THE MEADOW

In the middle of the woods, the Disney

Babies have found a lovely meadow filled

with  . Several animals have come

out to meet them. Baby Daisy is making friends

with a spotted  . Baby Donald

would like to have a race with the little

 who can run very fast. Someone

else would like to join them. It's the lively

 , who can jump, as well as run.

Up on a branch, looking over everything, sits

a with a bright red breast.

Fawn

Rabbit

Grasshopper

Clover

Robin

AT THE POND

The Disney Babies are playing near a pond

by a willow tree. They would like to feed

the beautiful white  . She lives there

with several other animals, including the

little green  sitting on the bank.

Poor Baby Gus has fallen into the pond, right

next to the  . The water isn't very deep,

so he will be all right. Baby Horace, Baby Gyro

and all the others are laughing at the

perched on Baby Gus's head. The frog thinks he

is sitting on a strange kind of  .

Turtle

Swan

Duck

Frog

Water Lily

ON THE MOUNTAIN

Baby Mickey and Baby Minnie have climbed

high up the mountain. They are surprised

to find so many animals. The  is

glad to see them, and calls the other

animals out of the woods. The  is

happy to pose for Minnie's camera, but the

 is somewhat shy. Many birds have

also come to see the Disney Babies. The

 with the curling feathers on their

heads are easy to see. So is the pretty

 with his long, colorful tail.

38

Bear

Moose

Wolf

Quails

Pheasant

WILD BABIES

Baby Donald has found the perfect treat for a

 . A pot of honey ! One of the other

wild babies thinks he might like some, too :

the red  behind the bear. Baby Daisy

is looking into a nest in a nearby tree and

sees a  looking back ! She is

pointing it out to the little raccoon, and to

Baby Pluto, who is barking at the  on

the pond. Baby Pete doesn't know why the little

 likes to chew wood. He's just tried

it, and it doesn't taste very good to him.

Bear Cub

Baby Bird

Fox Cub

Duckling

Beaver

AT THE FARMER'S MARKET

The Disney Babies enjoy seeing all the food

from the farm for sale at the Farmer's Market.

Baby Minnie likes the  of eggs, because

she helped find them. Baby Gus thinks the

watermelon is best, and Baby Goofy likes the

 because it can be carved into a jack-

o-lantern. Baby Mickey is pretending to sell

some  , as if he were in charge of the

stand. Would you rather buy an  ? Baby

Donald is laughing at Baby Pete, who fell into a

 of pickles trying to reach one !

Lettuce

Onion

Barrel

Pumpkin

Basket

AT NIGHTTIME

Night has fallen. The  are twinkling

in the dark sky, and a little light is reflected

by the  . The Disney Babies are curious

about all the night sounds. Listen ! Is that

the hoot of an  ? Baby Donald and Baby

Daisy don't know. Perhaps it was the high

squeak of the little  flying overhead.

Baby Mickey is enjoying himself with some new

friends. A little family of hedgehogs has arrived,

attracted by the golden light that shines

from Baby Mickey's  .

Moon

Stars

Bat

Owl

Lantern